IMAGES
of America

HOLLISTER

IMAGES
of America

HOLLISTER

Joseph M. McMahon and Peter Sonné

ARCADIA
PUBLISHING

Published by Arcadia Publishing
Charleston, South Carolina

Library of Congress Control Number: 2012935533

For all general information, please contact Arcadia Publishing:
Telephone 843-853-2070
Fax 843-853-0044
E-mail sales@arcadiapublishing.com
For customer service and orders:
Toll-Free 1-888-313-2665

Visit us on the Internet at www.arcadiapublishing.com

*I wish to dedicate this book to my wife, Leslie,
and grandchildren Jesse and Allison.
—Peter*

*I wish to thank my wife, Joanna, for her
patience and understanding.
—Joe*

CONTENTS

ACKNOWLEDGMENTS

A very special thanks to Debbie Norman and Greg and Stan Schmidt for contributing so much to make this book possible.

Thanks also goes to Francis Palmtag, Cliff Cardoza, Danny Corral, Mark Rianda, Janie Lausten, and Bill Hansen for allowing us access to their family photographs, archives, and all the details, without which this project would not have been possible.

Extra-special thanks to the San Benito County Historical Society and its president, Delbert Doty, for access to its photograph archives, which make up the main body of this book, and for preserving our local history.

Special thanks to Pat Hathaway's "California Views" for his assistance with photographs and information (caviews.com), and to Verona Flint, Aurelia Bozzo, and Wes Leiser for caring and taking the time to help with information and research.

We are indebted to the following for all the assistance, use of family photographs and archives, and the many emails that helped us gather a true history for chapter three: Deborah Norman and Gregory Schmidt with the help of Stanley Schmidt, Sharlene and Frank Van Rooy, Martha Bacon Miller, Clara Lou Melendy, Cynthia Melendy, and Alan Brookman.

INTRODUCTION

In order to understand the development of Hollister, it is necessary to know the history of the region. Fifteenth and largest in the chain of 21 missions built in New Spain by the Franciscan Friars, Mission San Juan Bautista was part of Spain's plan to colonize the country for protection against invasion by England, France, or Russia, because trading ships from these countries were making frequent appearances along the coast of California in the 18th century. As part of the master plan of Fr. Junipero Serra to locate the missions one day's walking distance apart, the padres received permission in 1795 from Mexico City to establish a mission between the San Carlos Borromeo de Carmelo and Santa Clara Missions, which were separated by 26 leagues (approximately 80 miles). A site was chosen along the San Benito River, and on June 24, 1797, the dedication of the new mission, named for St. John the Baptist, took place.

In 1820, the Mission San Juan Bautista owned over 40,000 head of cattle, nearly 1,400 tame horses, and about 70,000 head of sheep. Native Americans, under the control of the mission, employed more than 300 yoke of oxen in carrying on extensive farming operations. On August 17, 1833, the Mexican Congress passed a secularization law, effectively passing ownership of mission lands into the hands of private individuals. A large section of original mission property was granted to Rafael Gonzales in 1836 and was named Rancho San Justo. However, he quickly abandoned his claim to the land. In 1839, Gov. Juan Bautista Alvarado gave the land to Gen. Jose Castro, a local landowner. This grant consisted of 34,619 acres. General Castro fled California in 1850 at the time of statehood and sold the land to Don Francisco Pacheco for $1,400. In 1855, Flint, Bixby and Company bought the Rancho San Justo for $25,000, and the development of Hollister began.

Monterey County was one of the original counties in California when statehood was granted in 1850. In fact, Monterey was the capital of Spanish and Mexican California. In 1859, the state capital was moved to San Jose, and Monterey became the seat of Monterey County. By 1871, Monterey County was in the throes of a fight to move the county seat to a more centralized location in what was a large county. The communities of Castroville on the coast and Salinas in the valley competed with Monterey for the title of county seat. To add to the unrest, Hollister—with a population of around 2,000—began a movement to separate from Monterey and create a new county. There had always been some animosity between the people on the coast and the "people over the mountains," as Hollister was called.

A special election was held in 1872, at which time Salinas was selected as county seat, but the issue of division of the county into two was not settled at that time. The major issue was the selection of a seat of government for the new county. San Juan Bautista was the oldest and best known of the communities, but Hollister, with its larger population and its economic growth, was the better choice. The lines dividing the counties were created by Hollister businessmen, who ensured that Hollister would be the new county seat, since San Juan would be located too near to the lower end of the newly created county.

An act to create the County of San Benito and to establish the boundaries thereof was approved on February 12, 1874. By the terms of this act, the new county was carved out of territory formerly belonging to Monterey County, and Hollister was named the new county seat.

BIBLIOGRAPHY

Frusetta, Peter. *Quicksilver Country, California's New Idria Mining District*. Hollister: self-published.

———. *Beyond the Pinnacles*. King City, CA: Kasey Printing, 1989.

History of Monterey County California with Illustrations. San Francisco: Elliott and Moore Publishers, 1881.

Pierce, Marjorie. *East of the Gabilans*. Santa Cruz: Western Tanager Press, 1976.

San Benito County Superintendent of Schools. *San Benito County, Long Ago and Today*. Hollister: Office of the San Benito County Superintendent of Schools, 1959.

One

THE EARLY YEARS

The history of Rancho San Justo and the city of Hollister begins with two sheep drives to California in 1853. One of these drives was the Flint-Bixby drive, which was led by three young men from Maine: Dr. Thomas Flint, his brother Benjamin Flint, and their cousin Llewelyn Bixby. Col. William Welles Hollister, his brother Joseph Hollister, and their sister Lucy Brown led the other drive, which began in Ohio. Both drives took the southern route from Salt Lake to avoid early winter snows over the high passes of the Sierra Nevadas. The two parties met somewhere along the trail in Nevada, became acquainted, and came to California together.

On New Year's Day, 1854, Lucy Brown invited the Flints and Bixbys to dinner at the Hollister camp near San Bernadino, California, to celebrate their joint arrival to California. Their next meeting was held during the summer of 1855, when the Flints and Bixbys brought their sheep to the San Juan Valley for grazing and found that Colonel Hollister was already leasing pasture land on Rancho San Justo, a Mexican land grant consisting of 34,619 acres. Gov. Juan B. Alvarado had given this grant of land to Jose Castro in 1839. In 1850, Jose Castro sold the land to Don Francisco Pacheco after California became a state.

In October 1855, Flint, Bixby and Company bought Rancho San Justo from Pacheco for $25,000. Colonel Hollister agreed to buy one-half interest in the property. His sister Lucy Brown advanced the money, so the deed in 1858 was given in her name. She later deeded the land to her brother Colonel Hollister. Rancho San Justo was held in joint custody for three years until 1861, when the property was divided. Flint, Bixby and Company retained 13,000 acres, and Colonel Hollister retained 21,800 acres.

Hollister had taken the larger, eastern part of Rancho San Justo, while Flint-Bixby took the western part, including the San Juan Valley. Colonel Hollister married soon after the division of the rancho and selected a location to build a new house for his family and his sister. This site was near a small hill, today known as Park Hill. The site of the town was surveyed and laid out on November 19, 1868. The original plans divided the site into 50 homestead lots. The original town can be traced by following its boundary streets of North, South, East, and West. The east and west streets were numbered numerically with alleys named after prominent residents. Most rectangular lots backed into alleys and were 28 feet wide and 140 feet deep. Since this was a narrow lot, many buyers bought two or three adjoining lots that would allow for larger homes and barns. Corner lots sold for $200, while interior lots sold for $100. The first proposal was to call the young town San Justo, but Henry Hogan vehemently objected to all the "Sans" that were monopolizing names of the towns in the state and proposed the name Hollister, which was adopted.

In 1868, Colonel Hollister sold his portion of the rancho for $270,000 and moved his family to Santa Barbara. The buyers were a group of 50 men who called themselves the San Justo Homestead Association. On October 10, 1868, the San Justo Homestead Association formed for the purpose of purchasing and partitioning the land and was organized by the election of a board of directors. In 1876, the San Justo Homestead Association, having accomplished the object for which the association was organized, filed a petition for dissolution with the county clerk. On December 28, 1876, J.J. Harris, the county judge, signed a decree dissolving the corporation.

Pictured around 1910 is the interior of the Hollister freelance newspaper office, located at 630 San Benito Street in the Graham Meat Market building.

Pictured in 1884 is the Hollister freelance printing office, located in the Odd Fellows building on Fourth Street.

Seen here is the interior of Sousa's Harness shop, located at Fourth and East Streets. Manuel Enos is on the right, and John Machado is pictured with the horn around 1910.

Joe Harvey's grocery and dry goods store, shown here in early 1900, was located on the west-side corner of Third and San Benito Streets. Joe Harvey is behind the counter with unidentified patrons.

Pictured around 1910 are some unidentified local boys in an alleyway, staging a boxing event.

Around 1910, Peter Nielson stands in the center of Nielson Grocery Store in a coat and tie, sporting a mustache.

The old San Benito County Courthouse on Monterey Street between Fourth and Fifth Streets was constructed in 1888.

The Strittmatter Saloon was located on San Benito Street between Fifth and Fourth Streets. Within a year, that site would become the new Elks Building. The name of the saloon was later changed to the Old Corner Club.

Pictured is a view of downtown Hollister on July 4, 1898.

San Benito Street, Hollister, Cal.

Seen here is a view of San Benito Street looking south with the Rosenberg Brothers Store on right.

Sacred Heart Grammar School sustained considerable damage from the great earthquake of 1906. It was rebuilt and used for a number of years after.

Pictured is the business section of downtown Hollister after the 1906 earthquake.

The old Bell Theatre, shown in this c. 1925 photograph, was established in 1901 and was Hollister's first theater. Silent films were then a craze, with vaudeville slowly fading away into history.

Pictured around 1900 is the exterior of the Kelly Corner Saloon. A six-horse team is seen in front, pulling hay wagons.

The Bank of Hollister opened its doors in August 1874, and Thomas S. Hawkins was elected as its first president.

Seen here is a street view of the business district after the earthquake of 1906.

The Rosenberg Brothers General Store is pictured around the late 1890s or early 1900s with several two-horse hitch teams in front, each waiting to move ahead, possibly to hook onto small carts of dirt from roadwork being done or construction in the area. The store was established in 1874 and carried a large stock of goods.

Seen here is a view of San Benito Street around 1900.

Pictured around 1897 is "Blue Jay Hunt" William Sanchez on the left with "Doc" Bonnell on the right.

Pictured is the first San Benito County Office building with some of the first supervisors posing in front. From left to right are William McCarthay (court reporter), Charles Dowdy (deputy assessor), Vic McCray (county surveyor), George W. McConnell (deputy assessor), and Haydon Dowdy (first assessor). Dowdy was also involved in ranching in the south county, and in 1902, his son Elmer Dowdy became county recorder, holding that position for many years.

Pictured around 1910 is the courthouse square with the Briggs house in background, located at Fifth and Monterey Streets. Henry Briggs was the first secretary of the San Justo Homestead Association. The association paid Colonel Hollister $270,000 for the land, which was to become the town of Hollister.

Pictured in the late 1880s is East Street looking north along with the McKinnon Lumber Company in the large area to the left with the boxcar on the track. McKinnon Lumber Company has been in business since the mid-19th century and is still servicing the Hollister area today.

Seen here is Fifth Street looking west. Notice that the use of the horse and buggy has not completely vanished. One is parked behind a "horseless carriage" in this c. 1910 photo postcard.

Pictured around 1900 is the Farmers' and Merchants' Bank building. Located at the corner of Fifth and San Benito Streets, the building is still in use today with various office and retail space.

Pictured is a view of Fifth Street looking west around 1910. The Briggs house is first on the right, followed by the Thomas McMahon house and then the George Wapple house.

This rare 1869 photograph offers an early view of the business district along Fourth Street. Colonel Hollister's well-appointed home is seen on the far left, near what are now Fourth and Monterey Streets, which would be directly across from the present-day courthouse and sheriff's office. Colonel Hollister left the area in late 1868 or early 1869 with proceeds from the sale of his local holdings and profits from his sheep enterprise. He was bound for Santa Barbara, where he continued to prosper. The Montgomerys took over residency of the house, and at one point, it was turned into a boardinghouse.

This c. 1900 photograph looking west on Fourth Street shows the old Fremont School. There were 261 students registered in the school in 1881.

Pictured around 1900 is the Helvetia Hotel (formerly Charlie Mann's saloon and boardinghouse), located across San Benito Street from today's Bank of America. The Gila family ran the business for many years. Helvetia is the Latin term for Switzerland; the Gila family, from Switzerland, named the hotel for their native country.

The original Hazel Hawkins Memorial Hospital opened in 1907 and was built by Thomas S. Hawkins, one of the founders of Hollister.

The Walberg residence, located on Sixth and Monterey Streets, is one of many well-appointed residences in a growing neighborhood.

Pictured is the Banister residence, located at 500 Line Street. The apricot tree in the front center is blooming. The mildly warm temperatures in the spring and summer promoted the planting of many large apricot orchards in the area. San Benito County was known as the "Garden of the Apricot."

This is a photograph of "Bill," who was an interesting character in early San Benito County. Ishmael "Bill" Williams was born around 1835 as a slave for the N.W. Hicks family in Georgia and came to California during the Civil War. Bill held the hauling contract for the New Idria Mines in the mid-1870s and drove a 10-horse jerk-line team over the tortuous, 50-mile route to Tres Pinos, where the 76-pound iron flasks of mercury were unloaded at the railroad docks and shipped all over the United States.

Thomas McCloskey, George Wapple's father-in-law, pauses his buggy on Monterey Street with the San Benito County Courthouse in the background in the late 1880s.

Shown is the Hollister City Hall building on Fifth Street. The structure is still in use today as the town's city hall.

Sacred Heart Church, with its prominent steeple, has been a landmark for many years. Thomas McMahon donated the land for the church. His wife, Isabel, was the daughter of Margaret and Patrick Breen of the Donner Party.

South Street in winter looking West, Hollister, Cal.

Shown is a winter scene of South Street looking west.

The Hollister High School hose cart team would compete in cart races on various holidays, such as the Fourth of July, with other teams from neighboring towns. It was always a crowd pleaser. The school was constructed on the former site of the William Palmtag residence. Palmtag was a prominent liquor dealer who came to Hollister in 1872 and established a liquor and cigar business. He was also involved in local politics and banking.

The George Wapple residence is pictured on the corner of Fifth and West Streets.

J.M. Brown built the Hollister Flouring Mill in 1870. It was not in constant operation until 1879, when it was purchased by Shakelford and Hinds, who overhauled the business and added new machinery. At its peak, it had a capacity of 140 barrels a day.

The Hodges house was located on Fourth Street between Monterey and West Streets. It became a boardinghouse in 1910 and was later used by the Methodist Church.

The residence of Benjamin Flint Gould was built around 1870 by J.M. Brown, who also built the first flour mill in Hollister.

Naderman's Model Bakery was built in 1888. Pictured are Maria Naderman on the right and Ed Naderman in the center. The Nadermans lived upstairs, while the ovens and cooking stoves were down in the basement and the retail space was at street level.

The Beehive Men's Clothiers was located on San Benito Street. The first man on the left in this c. 1900 photograph is Judge Dooling.

The San Benito County Courthouse was built in 1888.

Shown is the interior of the San Benito Trading Company along with an unidentified man.

Pictured is Monterey Street in 1902, as seen from Park Hill. The large building with the high steeple to the right is the county courthouse. The Fashion Stables are visible on the left with a large false front.

Two

Tres Pinos and Paicines

The small community of Paicines, 12 miles south of Hollister, was originally known as Tres Pinos for three pines that once stood on the bank of a creek. By 1866, the settlement had a general store that was owned by the Sepulveda brothers of Baja California. When the railroad was extended south of Hollister to handle freight from the New Idria Mines, a town grew up around the new station. This railhead was six miles northwest of the village and, for some reason, was also called Tres Pinos. Eventually, the old village south of the station became known as Paicines, a name derived from the Constanoan Indian village of Pagsin, which was located in that region. Today, the names Tres Pinos and Paicines refer to separate communities.

Tres Pinos today is a shadow of its former self. It was once a prosperous center of trade for hay, grain, and cattle. This part of San Benito County was all ranching and farming, and it was noted for the quality of its grain and hay. Wagons piled high with hay were pulled by double teams of horses that would depart from Tres Pinos for various parts of the country. The Southern Pacific Railroad Company put the railroad through in 1873 and built a station on the site. When the trains came, Tres Pinos became a central shipping point for grain and cattle from the many ranches in the county. The railroad was also the terminal for the stage line and express, owned by A.G. Fruitts, from the New Idria Mines. From this station, quicksilver was shipped out of the county to parts all over the nation. However, in 1944, the railroad discontinued its run to Tres Pinos and dismantled the station. The town began to decline, and when the old Southern Pacific Hotel was torn down, Tres Pinos became a small relic of its former days.

In its heyday, Paicines had a school, hotel, blacksmith shop, and saddler. Mule teams frequently came through town en route to the railhead in Tres Pinos form the New Idria quicksilver mines. All that remains of this once-bustling community is a general store and a small post office.

A map showing Hollister, Tres Pinos, and the Paicines region of the county depicts the locations of the original Mexican land grants. (Courtesy Marjorie Pierce.)

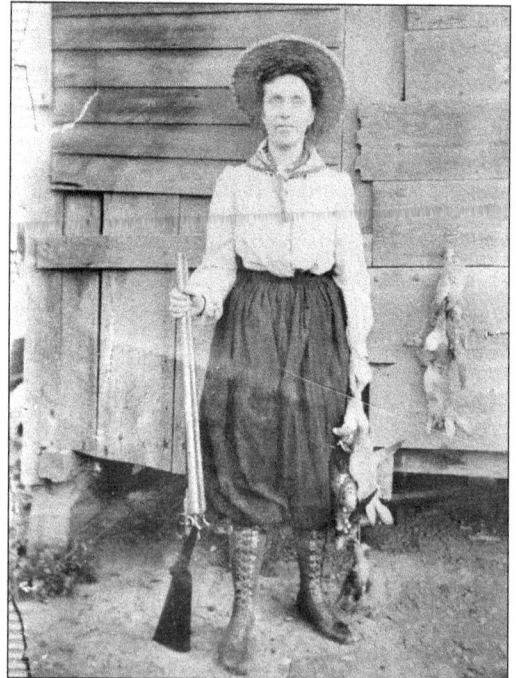

Sadie Hain Parker of south San Benito County finds the time to pose in this c. 1900 photograph with her double-barrel shotgun, which she used on what appears to be a successful hunting trip. Note the high-top, lace-up boots, a style of footwear that, among other things, came in handy to protect the wearer's leg from rattlesnake bite. Rattlers are very common in the warm, south county hill area.

The Hain family gathers in this 1900 photograph. The site of this photograph was the bridge that crossed over the Bear Valley Creek on the Arthur L. Hain Ranch. Flora (Hain) Harter stands with her hand on the pump that furnished water for Arthur's home, which was situated nearby. From left to right are Frank Hain, Sadie Hain, Mary Hain, Flora Harter, Carrie Hain, Arthur Hain, unidentified, Schuyler C. Hain, Mary Ann Hain, and John Hain Sr.

Cousins from the Laustens and Hain family pose for this c. 1940 photograph. Both sides of the family had homesteaded the south county area in the later part of the 19th century, helping develop it into a prosperous ranching community that contributed so much in the development of Hollister and Tres Pinos. From left to right are unidentified, Sidney "Bud" Lausten, Ann Hain, Kenneth Lausten, and unidentified.

Various unidentified residents of the Bear Valley area in South San Benito County pose for this community picnic photograph around 1910. Note the milk can near the bottom center, which has "Tres Pinos" hand-printed on its side. Tres Pinos was just south of Hollister and was home to the terminus of the Southern Pacific Railroad (SPRR). The SPRR put down track at Tres Pinos to accommodate the large quantities of grain, cattle, and other products being raised in the south county. From this point, it was shipped back through Hollister to various parts of the United States. At one time, the south county was one of largest grain and hay producers in the country.

Joseph Rianda Jr. and his family were photographed in 1929 at their home in Tres Pinos.

Joseph Rianda was born in Switzerland on August 16, 1858. At the age of 19, he landed in San Francisco on July 4, 1877. He spent a very short time in San Francisco before heading to Watsonville, California. From there, he moved to the Salinas Valley and took up farming on the Catherine Ranch, where he worked for six years. In 1884, Joseph came to Tres Pinos and opened a general merchandise store, remaining in business for over 40 years. He also owned two ranches in the area and was postmaster for many years at the Tres Pinos post office.

Shown in this c. 1920 photograph is the interior of Rianda's General Store in Tres Pinos, California. Joseph Rianda Sr. and his daughter Elvizia Rianda (Mederios) are pictured. Elvizia was born 1894.

Joseph Rianda is the second man from left, Joene Rianda is the little boy, and next to him is Parcilla Rianda, his mother. The man on far right is Acquillino Rianda, nephew of Joseph Rianda Sr., who died at the age of 28. The others are unidentified.

Pictured around 1909 is the Tres Pinos Band. Joseph Rianda Jr. is fifth from right. The rest of the band is unidentified. They were a very popular group and played in the Tres Pinos and Paicines area for various events.

Shown is the interior of the Etcheverry Hotel (originally called the Southern Pacific Hotel) in Tres Pinos in 1940. Frank Laveroni is second from the left, and on the far right is hotel manager John Barcelone, leaning on the counter. The other three patrons are unidentified.

Pictured around 1910 is Rianda's General Store with Joseph Rianda Sr. standing in the doorway. The others are unidentified. Rianda's General Store became a partnership, which eventually included a barbershop, an eatery, a saloon, and an inventory building. The year 1910 was good for business in Tres Pinos and Hollister, because one-fifth of California's hay crop passed through the towns' depots that year.

Two eight-mule jerk line teams are pictured around 1910 on Main Street in Paicines. These teams hauled flasks of quicksilver from the New Idria Mines to the railhead in Tres Pinos and returned with supplies for the mines. The 60-mile trip from Tres Pinos to the mines was filled with all sorts of hazards, such as landslides, rattlesnakes spooking the teams, and bandits. The most well-known of the bandits, Tiburcio Vasquez, roamed the area for a number of years and pulled his final job at Tres Pinos in Snyder's Store, resulting in the death of several people who were simply in the wrong place at the wrong time. This would be Vasquez's downfall, as he was hunted down and stood trial in San Jose, where he was found guilty and hanged.

Members of the Paicines baseball team are, from left to right, (first row) Clair Ingram and Frank McGrury; (second row) Frank Hooton and Robert Matthews; (third row) Albert Carmack, John Ingles, Rayner Matthews, Glen Stevens, and Edward Hooton.

Pictured around 1910 is a common scene of threshing hay with a steam tractor near Tres Pinos.

This 1909 photograph postcard shows the Fruits home in Tres Pinos. The residence is still standing today.

Pictured in 1895 is the Frank Muder residence in Tres Pinos. Pictured from left to right are Mrs. Frank Muder (Mary), Naomi Brown, "Auntie" Bonnell, and Leonora Muder, holding her doll.

Miners are pictured in the late 1930s heading into one of the mine shafts at the New Idria Mines. The area of land where New Idria is located was purchased by San Benito County from Merced and Fresno Counties as part of a 2,000-acre deal in 1887. This particular section was initially located in what was then Fresno County. The mission fathers discovered the mine in 1825, and they first found the ore to be cinnabar. The mine was named New Idria for the Idria Mine in Austria. Work began at the mine in 1853. In 1861, there were 200 to 300 men working there.

New Idria Mine gave the world over half of its quicksilver since it was opened. It was one of the oldest mines in America and the second largest quicksilver mine in the world. Miners and their families lived in houses furnished by the company. Workers without families lived in a dormitory and had their meals in a dining hall. There was a school, general store, post office, and other buildings and businesses that were needed to serve the community. From one of the tunnels, $4 million in quicksilver was mined. New Idria was open for over 100 years until it closed down in 1974. This c. 1930 photograph shows miners inside the shaft. San Benito County had other mines in operation in the 19th century that produced other precious metals. Some of the mine names and districts were the Indicate Mine, the Sleeping Beauty Mine, the Forbes Mine, the McLeod Mine, the Central Quartz Mining District, Eagle Mine, and the Alta Quartz Mining District.

Paicines Feed Stable was operated in conjunction with the Paicines Hotel. The outside stairway led to a dance hall, which was about 35 feet by 70 feet. Most Saturday nights, a dance was held that was attended by many of the area's residents. Rob Reno, a barber in Tres Pinos, and Lew Crosby, also from Tres Pinos, usually furnished the music. The barn section held about 30 horses, which were kept on the right, and the buggies went through the open doorway at the left.

Shown here is the Paicines General Store and post office in the mid-1950s.

Pictured is the Paicines General Store in the early 1910s.

Shown is a 1910 photo postcard of the Tres Pinos School.

Seen is a photograph of Paicines Hotel, built around 1870. It served as a busy stopping-off spot for many years. It was also the location of one of the fatalities in connection with the Vasquez gang during the course of a robbery across the street at Snyder's Store in 1872. The victim, Leander Davidson, was struck and killed by a stray bullet that passed through the front doors and found its mark in Davidson's body. Vasquez and his gang were hunted down for several killings in connection with the robbery. Vasquez was hanged at San Jose in 1875.

Extracting coal in San Benito County was another form of mining that took place in the later part of the 19th century and into the first part of the 20th century. As seen in this photo postcard, miners take a moment from the hard work of coal mining to pose before heading back into the hole.

HOLLISTER COAL CO., HOLLISTER. CAL.

Apricot picking and cutting has seen the likes of many San Benito County youth over many decades. Kids will always be kids, even at cutting time, as seen in this mid-1950s photograph taken on the Hain Ranch in Tres Pinos. From left to right are Ralph, Janie, Carol, and Nancy Lausten pausing for a cold watermelon break on a warm day, which brought the big smiles.

Ann (Hain) Lausten (left) and Martha Jane Wier take a break from gardening in this early-1930s photograph on the Hain Ranch in Tres Pinos. The young lady in the middle is not identified. Ann went on to become the first full-time female employee at the Pinnacles National Monument, whose eastern entrance is located in the south county and is the one used most by tourists from all over the world. Ann's great-uncle Schuyler Hain was instrumental in getting the Pinnacles set aside as a national monument.

In 1870, the Southern Pacific Railroad laid its first track from Carnardero (about three miles south of Gilroy) to Hollister. The tracks were extended south to Tres Pinos by 1873. Hay, grain, cattle, and ore were shipped out by rail to all points of importance. The Tres Pinos depot saw a great deal of activity and played a major role in the building of Hollister's future.

The Church of the Immaculate Conception was built in 1894 on land donated by Juan Etcheverry.

The Mulberry Hotel and General Store was owned and operated by George M. Lawton and his wife, Eliza. They opened the business after moving to the Mulberry area shortly after the earthquake of 1906. George was born in San Francisco and died when he fell off the hotel roof in 1916. The young man on the left may be George Lawton Jr.

Pictured is Marcom's General Store in Tres Pinos. This well-stocked store was one of several in Tres Pinos. It was known that if an item could not be found at Marcom's, one would have to go without it.

Pictured here are five-horse teams pulling hay wagons at Tres Pinos and heading to the Southern Pacific Depot.

The Old Southern Pacific Hotel was located in Tres Pinos. This photograph dates to the late 1930s, when it was known as the Etcheverry Hotel.

Tres Pinos today is not as populated as it was 100 years ago, and most of its buildings have vanished with the passing of time. Some, such as the 19th Hole, still remain in business after 130 years of serving the public. It is an authentic Old West saloon and eatery that has seen many generations come and go, and is also a place where one can still see bullet holes from a Colt .45 peeking out into the main barroom.

Another historic structure still being used is the old Lathrop Grain and Hay Company building, which has the drive-on scale in front. In the early days, teams of horses would pull large freight wagons to the site, where they were loaded with grain and hay. They would be weighed and then continue on to the depot. The Tres Pinos Ranch Supply calls it home today.

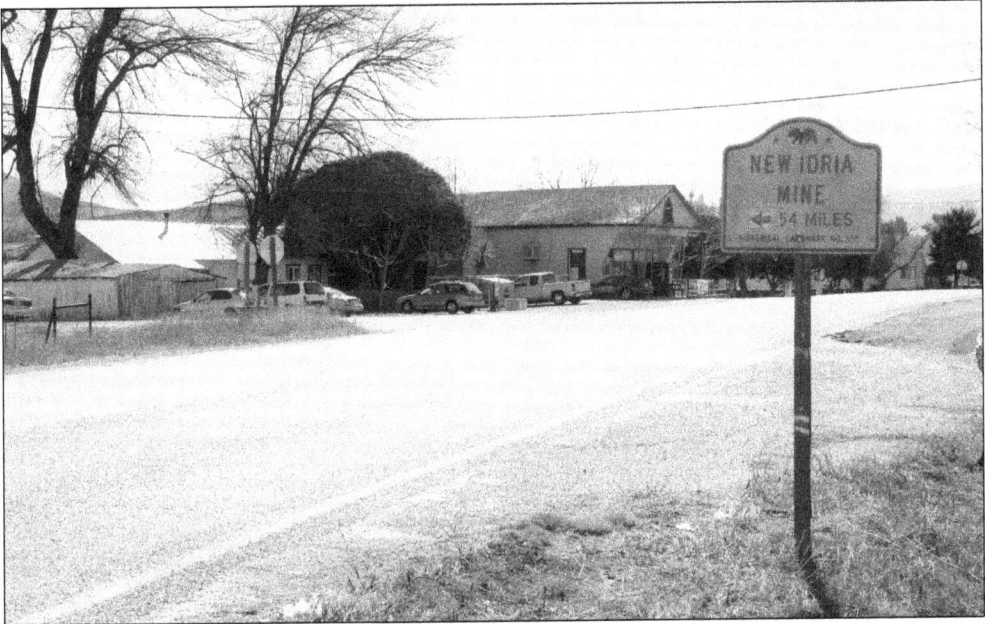

The only remaining business in Paicines today is the General Store and Cafe. To the rear of the store is the US Post Office. As the sign indicates, the New Idria Mine is off to the left down Panoche Road. Not much remains of the mine area today other than a few small structures. Several fires have destroyed most of the buildings and what remained of the mill itself over the last 40 years. The once-busy mining town with a school, church, stores, doctors, bandits, and people is nothing more now than a memory that is a part of San Benito County's rich history.

Onionskin paper from Joseph Rianda's general store order book was sent to the Levi Strauss Company in San Francisco to place an order. The store was located at the corner of Fourth Street and what is now Highway 25. The site is presently a parking lot next to the post office.

Pictured is a 1958 stock certificate from the New Idria Mining and Chemical Company, issued for 100 shares at 50¢ each. The mine was in operation for over 100 years. (Collection of Peter Sonné.)

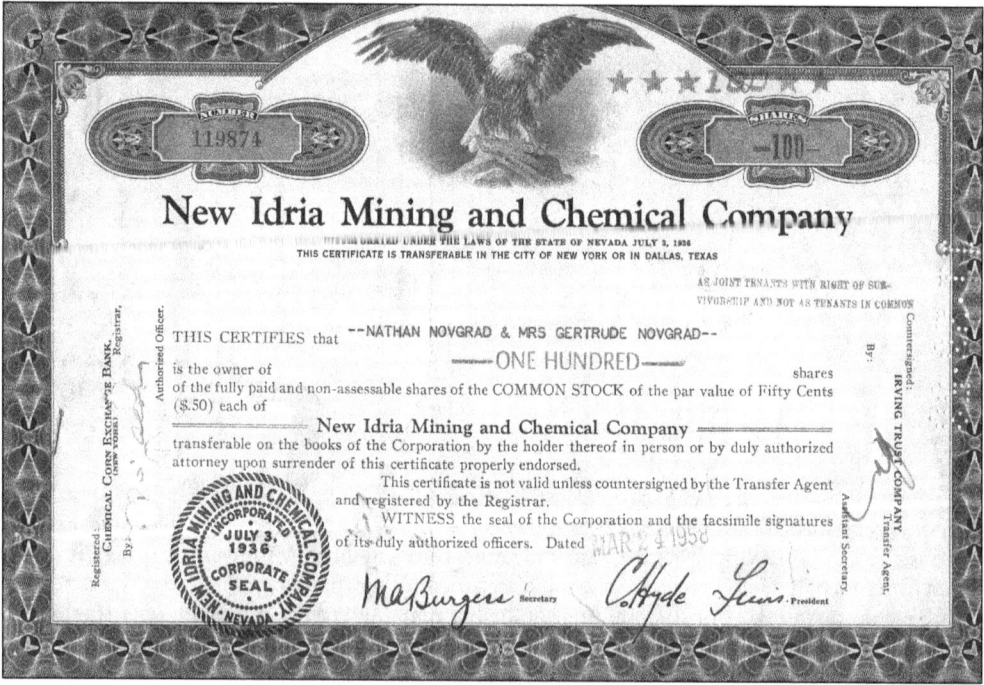

Three

THE PINNACLES REGION

The region around Pinnacles National Monument in the southern Gabilan Range originally was known as Chalone, named for the tribe of Costanoan Indians who called it home. The San Benito River and Chalone Creek run through the oak-studded hills and valleys, which are fractured by four large earthquake faults, including the San Andreas. In 1791, when Spanish padres opened Mission Nuestra Señora de la Soledad, some 900 Chalone lived in villages throughout this territory. Over the next 25 years, the Spanish mission system disrupted their trading, food, and social networks, and they migrated to Soledad, leaving the region barely populated for decades.

The only pre-1848 land grant in the surrounding region was San Lorenzo, awarded to Mexican government official Rafael Sanchez in 1846 for stock range. In 1856, when diarist Ygnacio Pedro Villegas traveled through on his way to Santa Barbara, he encountered a single family between Paicines and King City. With the passage of the Homestead Act in 1862, people once again settled the Pinnacles region. By 1880, the population, including the communities of Willow Creek, Bear Valley, San Benito, and Bitterwater, had grown to 1,600 people from all over the United States, Canada, Mexico, and Europe. They dry-farmed vegetables, hay, and grain and raised draft horses, beef, dairy cattle, goats, swine, poultry, and bees. They also planted apple, apricot, and pear orchards, experimented with wine grapes and silkworm culture, and mined quicksilver. Lack of water and competition from large-scale, irrigated agriculture in the Salinas and Pajaro Valleys gradually reduced the number of viable farms. Today, the region is home to 650 people.

The signature geological feature of the landscape is the Pinnacles National Monument, a 23.5-million-year-old volcanic formation that has moved north from Los Angeles nearly 200 miles along the San Andreas Fault. Early English-speaking settlers called the formation the Big Rock Pile. Spanish-speaking settlers called the spectacular spires Los Peñascos de la Gloria, or Crags of Heaven. By the 1890s, the names Palisades and Pinnacles were commonly used. With the creation of the national monument in 1908 by Pres. Theodore Roosevelt, the name Pinnacles became official.

State Highway 25 replaced the stage road through the San Benito River Valley from Hollister to the now-defunct village of San Benito, once a contender for the San Benito County seat. According to an 1873 schedule, the stage left Hollister at 7:30 a.m. and reached San Benito at 5:00 p.m., a 33-mile journey. Drivers traveled southbound on Mondays, Wednesdays, and Fridays and returned north on the following days. Once a week, the stage continued south to the Picacho quicksilver mines and on to Peachtree, where cattle baron Henry Miller had a large ranch. This photograph shows the San Benito stage around 1890.

Settlers built the one-room Bear Valley School on the ranch of Dr. Americus Powers, the area's first physician, in 1873. The first teacher was P. Troy, and the trustees were William K. Bacon, George M. Butterfield, and John T. Prewett. A larger schoolhouse, shown in this c. 1900 photograph, was built in the 1890s. Bear Valley School graduated its first eighth-grade class in 1899. The school closed in 1952, but the building continued as a community center, hosting church services; state and county elections; Farm Bureau, 4-H, and Home Department meetings; card parties; dances; family gatherings; baseball games; and World War II military drills. The National Park Service acquired the former school in 2011. (Courtesy Stanley Schmidt and Martha Bacon Miller.)

Outdoor play was an important part of the day at Bear Valley School. During morning and afternoon recesses, the teacher supervised games of baseball, catch, and tag. In this photograph, taken around 1916 or 1917, students from left to right are George Butterfield, Everett Prewett, Evelyn Prewett, Grace Butterfield, Lois Hain, Viella Butterfield, Carol Prewett, and Winnie Krueger. (Photograph by Anna Guidinger Melendy, courtesy Catherine C. Melendy.)

The village of San Benito got its start in the 1860s. By 1868, Robert Beasley's merchandise store and John Shell's blacksmith shop were open for business. In 1871, Wiley Williams opened the San Benito Hotel and Saloon. All of these enterprises were purchased by Illinois native Allen Leonard, who arrived in 1872 and became the virtual proprietor of the town. When San Benito County formed in 1874, San Benito was a contender for the county seat, but it lost out to Hollister.

Bear Valley families gathered in 1890, having traveled in spring wagons to summertime picnics on the ground in the shade of spreading native valley oaks. Picnics were popular, especially on Sundays, Memorial Day, and the Fourth of July. On the Fourth, the day's events included patriotic oratory, singing, and a reading of the Declaration of Independence.

During the summer, fruit and vegetable peddlers traveled up and down the San Benito River selling produce, such as strawberries, apricots, and apples, which provided a treat in the baskets of food contributed by each family. In this 1921 photograph, descendants of the same Bear Valley families gathered, having traveled to the picnic grounds in automobiles. (Courtesy Stanley Schmidt.)

The Homestead Act of 1862 allowed settlers to claim 160 acres of farmland for a small filing fee. Homesteaders were required to be at least 21 years old (or married, if younger) and had to live on the land for five years while making improvements, such as building a house and fencing the land. A tent often provided shelter until the house was ready. This photograph shows the Jonathan Jones family some time in the 1890s. Jones received a patent on his claim in 1902. (Photograph by Oliver Bacon, courtesy Martha Bacon Miller.)

A traveling photographer, who spent a week photographing homes and families in Bitterwater in mid-January 1878, took this tintype of the David Munson Selleck homestead. (Photograph by a Mr. Disney, courtesy Gregory and Stanley Schmidt.)

Educator Horace Greeley Bacon and his wife, Nettie Smith, settled on a ranch east of the Bear Valley School after their marriage in 1891. Bacon taught all grades at the one-room Bear Valley School for 20 years. In this c. 1895 photograph, he and Nettie pose with their children Edith (left) and Clarence (in Nettie's arms).

In 1904, Bacon became chairman of the San Benito County Board of Education, and at that time, he and Nettie replaced their homestead cabin with a larger house, pictured here. The place burned in the 1960s in a fire sparked by an electric transformer. (Photograph by Oliver Bacon, courtesy Stanley Schmidt.)

Several small mining operations cropped up near the Pinnacles in the late 19th and early 20th centuries. With the California Gold Rush of 1849 and Nevada's Comstock silver strike of 1859 still within recent memory, individuals sought gold, silver, and copper, though none was found in any significant quantities. More promising were showings of cinnabar, or quicksilver, though miners were disappointed that local mines yielded nothing like the rich deposits found at New Almaden, 75 miles to the north, and New Idria, 50 miles to the southeast. (Photograph by Oliver Bacon, courtesy Martha Bacon Miller.)

This 1890s photograph, taken at a homestead near the Pinnacles, shows construction typical of the place and time. The house is roofed with layered planks, probably redwood from neighboring Santa Cruz County, and is enclosed with hand-hewn logs. The nearest sources of milled lumber were some 50 miles away over rough terrain, so homesteaders built with available materials and later replaced them when they had the means.

The shed in this photograph, which was taken on the Jonathan Jones homestead at the Pinnacles, shows how it was framed with logs and roofed with brush. The roof is sturdy enough to hold the four individuals seated on it. In front of the shed is a brush fence. As a matter of expediency, homesteaders built livestock corrals and fences of packed brush interwoven with vines and staked with peeled logs. (Photograph by Oliver Bacon, courtesy Martha Bacon Miller.)

As the surrounding population grew, so did the renown of the spectacular scenery at the Pinnacles, where condors soared above the peaks, and the banks of Chalone Creek offered a green haven for picnickers and hikers. Brothers Oliver and Benjamin Bacon, shown here in the 1890s with hikers, were early guides. Even before the Pinnacles became a national monument, the Hollister Stationers sold scenic postcards to visitors, and the Mulberry Hotel—some 13 miles north of the Pinnacles—offered lodging.

During the 1890s, when this photograph was taken, the Pinnacles was also known as the Palisades. Visitors found hospitality with local ranchers, who encouraged public access. (Photograph by Oliver Bacon, courtesy Martha Bacon Miller.)

Elizabeth Shell Bacon (left) and her daughter-in-law Nettie Smith Bacon (right) pose on a handmade wooden footbridge over Bear Valley Creek (now known as Sandy Creek) some time in the 1890s. Large predators, such as grizzly bears, mountain lions, and coyotes, were a common sight when settlers arrived in the region. (Photograph by Oliver Bacon, courtesy Martha Bacon Miller.)

Bear Valley ranchers switched from horse to steam power in 1891, when rancher John T. Prewett purchased the steam engine shown in this photograph. The engine was powered by burning wood or straw, and a fire-arrester at the top of the smoke stack kept sparks from escaping and igniting the fuel supply, which was pulled in a wagon behind the engine. (Courtesy Stanley Schmidt.)

Bear Valley's first post office opened on March 30, 1894, with rancher Schuyler Hain as postmaster. The office itself was located in the home of his brother Arthur Hain. In 1924, the name was changed to Pinnacles. The post office was discontinued in July 1953. This photograph of the Arthur Hain home was taken around 1900. (Photograph by Oliver Bacon, courtesy Martha Bacon Miller.)

The Willow Creek Cemetery was established in the 1870s as a burial ground for neighboring ranches. The earliest known burial was Clinton Smith, age two, who died in 1877. The inscription on his stone reads, " 'Tis a little grave, but O have care for worldwide hopes are buried there: How much of light, how much of joy is buried with a darling boy." In 1904, ranchers George and Elizabeth Kelly Melendy leased the land and began maintaining the cemetery. The stone in this photograph commemorates Orange C. Modie (1859–1887), the son of a pioneer Willow Creek family who came west over the Donner Pass around 1849, carrying two of their littlest children in saddlebags. The inscription reads, "I would not give my hope of Heaven for a thousand worlds like this." (Photograph by John Dennis Cooper.)

Dr. Americus Windsor Powers was the first physician to practice in the Pinnacles region. This photograph is a copy of a daguerreotype made in Sheboygan, Wisconsin, in 1856, just before the doctor moved his family to California. In 1865, Powers, his nephew Henry Melendy, and his brother-in-law Aaron Rockwood became the first settlers in Bear Valley, where they raised Thoroughbred horses. (Courtesy Deborah Melendy Norman.)

Because ranches were far apart and homes were small, young people socialized at outdoor gatherings during nice weather. This photograph was taken by William K. Bacon—one of Bear Valley School's first trustees—and includes members of many early ranching families who farmed near the Pinnacles. Hunting was a favorite pastime, and young men usually carried rifles in case they spotted a deer, since venison was a staple of the dinner table. (Photograph by William K. Bacon, courtesy Sara May DeRosa.)

Settlers heated their homes and fueled smokehouses with limbs harvested from nearby stands of native valley, coast, and blue oak. (Photograph by Oliver Bacon, courtesy Martha Bacon Miller.)

Four

HOLLISTER

The development of Hollister began in 1874, when the city was officially incorporated; it had secured its place as the most important city in the region around the time San Benito County was formed. The hay industry brought growth and prosperity, and the coming of the railroad brought increased communication from the rest of the world. Hollister became famous as the "Hay City," and successful families began building splendid new homes that would reflect their position in society. Taking a walk through downtown will provide a glimpse of Hollister in its heyday. The downtown area, which was listed in the National Registry of Historic Places in 1993, represents the pre–World War II character of the years from 1880 to 1942, with architectural styles including Italianate, Gothic Revival, Greek, Neoclassical, and Mediterranean.

The town of Hollister has the dubious distinction of having been built directly on top of an active creeping fault, the Calaveras Fault, which branches off from the San Andreas Fault about 20 miles south of town. Geographically speaking, however, Hollister may be one of the safest places to be in the western United States. The probability of a strong earthquake in the next 50 years is very low—less than 30 percent—because the segment that runs through the town and San Benito County does not appear to be prone to large jolts. The fault just creeps along with constant activity, taking away the probability of a large quake. Evidence of this "fault creep" can be seen on offset sidewalks and cracked bulkheads throughout town.

The principal economic activities of the area are agriculture, manufacturing, and tourism. Baby salad lettuce continues to be the county's number-one crop, closely followed by other row crops, such as tomatoes and peppers. Apricots, cherries, and walnuts continue to be grown around Hollister, while the cattle industry can be found in the drier, southern portion of the county. Pinnacles National Monument in the southern part of the county, San Juan Bautista State Historical Park, Fremont Peak State Park, Hollister Hills State Vehicular Recreation Area, and the many wineries bring visitors into the area year-round.

With its quality of life, temperate year-round climate, remarkable variety of landscapes, and proximity to the myriad recreational, educational, and cultural opportunities of Central California, Hollister and San Benito County is a wonderful place to call home.

In this September 1904 photograph, Viola Dunne, wife of local businessman James Dunne, is sitting behind the wheel of the family's automobile, showing guests around San Benito County. Seated in the rear to the right is Anita McCarthy of Cork, Ireland, and next to her is a Miss Hall. The Dunnes owned the San Felipe Rancho near Pacheco Pass, about 20 miles northeast of Hollister.

Henry Wright poses behind his well-appointed bar in this late-19th-century photograph. There is a sign just above his head, resting on the shelf, that reads, "Buttermilk 5 cents." The bar was located in the Muder building, which is now Cheap Seats Café at 427 San Benito Street. After Henry Wright installed his bar, a tobacco shop, the Smokehouse, did business for many years. A brothel on the second floor was in business until the early 1950s.

In this May 1923 photograph, local fruit and vegetable vendor Fred Rist hams it up in front of a large poster promoting the western film *The Covered Wagon*, which was showing at the Opal Theatre. Rist also has small promotional posters on his peddler's wagon, which had a cabin built over the old wagon. Looking closely, it is obvious that he is playing up the part by carrying a holstered revolver.

Frank Muder poses in front of the Muder building at 427 San Benito Street with the Smokehouse tobacco shop in background. This building still stands, and the sports bar Cheap Seats is its present occupant. The Hollister Cyclery is visible to the left.

On March 18, 1914, the Hollister Civic Club poses with Hollister High School students during a lunch break. They were planting trees a mile and a half north outside of town as a beautification project.

The old Hollister Brewery is shown in this c. 1910 photograph with two carloads of visitors parked out front. The horseless carriage on the left is a Mitchell. The brewery was located where the Veterans' Building is now. The building on the left still stands today. The top floor contained apartments, and on the first floor was a business. Today, the Hard Times Café calls the first floor home.

Shown is a 1971 photograph taken
from Park Hill looking southwest.
The steeple of Sacred Heart Church
is visible just to the center right.

Pictured in the mid-1950s is the Penny
Wise Drugstore on San Benito Street.

The Granger's Union Hardware and Grocer was built in 1886 at a cost of $28,000. The Granger's Union Company could be depended on to sell "anything the farmer needs," plus some. In addition to the items named in the large roof sign, buyers could find carpets, clothing, farm equipment, and cars.

This photograph was taken in the summer of 1891 at Charles Henry Wagner's Cash Grocer, which was complete with a delivery wagon and driver parked out front. It is believed that Charles Wagner is the man pictured in the center wearing a suit with his right hand on his hip.

In this early-1900s photograph, workers are sending locally grown apricots through a new machine known as an "Apricot Pitter." The machine was not very popular and never succeeded. The area was known for its high-producing orchards of Blenheim apricots.

This wonderful 1909 photograph of the UPEC, a Portuguese fraternal lodge, was taken in front of the old Fremont School on Fourth Street across from the old courthouse. Seated on the bottom row, third from the right, is Manuel F. Machado Cardoza. Unfortunately, the others are not identified.

The Hollister Southern Pacific train depot is pictured in 1913. The building is still standing today and is used by several commercial businesses.

In this c. 1932 photograph, employees of the India Tire Company pose for a photograph. It was located at Fourth and East Streets and was owned by the Filice family. It later became an Oldsmobile dealership, then a liquor store, and is now occupied by San Benito Glass.

Shown is a parade celebrating the Diamond Jubilee, the 75th anniversary of the founding of the City of Hollister. The IOOF is pictured with its float being pulled along by a new DeSoto. Whalen's Drugs is in the background on the corner of the building with the stripped awnings. This photograph was taken in August 1947, just one month after the famous motorcycle event in July, during which the town of Hollister was temporally shut down by a group of unruly motorcyclists who came to watch the motorcycle races. The incident led to the making of the film *The Wild One*, starring Marlon Brando and Lee Marvin.

Pictured is San Benito Street looking south. Wapple Drugs and the Bank of Italy (which later became Bank of America) are visible on the right in the early-1920s postcard.

Pictured around 1900 is the Gold Nugget Butter Company with a delivery wagon on the left, carrying a load of cream in cans to be delivered.

The Hollister Eagles Drum Corps pose after a performance.

Hollister Eagles Drum Corps, Aerie 1017 won many competitions around the state. In the 1940s, it had just won first place in a Fourth of July parade at Redwood City, which had been observed by the captain of the USS *Hollister* destroyer. He was so impressed that he asked the unit to play aboard the *Hollister*, which was moored at the dock near the old cement plant at Redwood City. They did, and they won more applause.

The Jones and Arnold Garage Chevrolet dealer offers expert mechanics on duty in this c. 1924 photograph.

This 1920s photograph shows the Jones and Arnold Chevrolet Garage with three new Chevy school buses for San Benito High School parked in front.

Pictured is a drying yard, where fruit was placed in trays to dry in the sun. The Smith family stands in the background. For decades, many local school kids who were old enough to work and wanted to earn money spent many summers cutting "cots" in the sheds on local farms. San Benito County was known as the Blenheim apricot capital of the world.

In this 1903 photograph, Fred Hawkins Sr. (left) and August Wehmueller pose while dipping prunes and then spreading them on trays for drying. The basket used for the dipping process was used until 1910. The prunes were dipped into hot water and lye over a fire, which was kept burning with fruitwood. The Wehmueller prune orchard in the background was planted in 1891 at Line Street and Apricot Lane. The orchard was converted into apricots in the 1930s, and as late as 1968, it was still intact. Now, it is all gone and is currently a residential area.

Pictured is the Hollister High football team around 1937. Joe Rianda Jr. is the second row, third from left (number 8).

Workers from the Victor Flour Mills take a moment to pose for this c. 1887 group photograph. One of the only people who are clearly identified is Will Steinbeck (fifth from left), who is standing and wearing a suit with a watch chain in his vest. Steinbeck was an uncle to author John Steinbeck. Standing in the wagon wearing a hat with coat and vest just above Steinbeck is Gordon Foote, the company clerk.

San Benito Shell Service Station was located on San Felipe Road, just north of Hollister, in this mid-1930s photograph. The station was doing a steady business with the increase of vehicle traffic coming into Hollister as well as business and residential growth. The attendant is unknown, but he busy fueling a customer's auto with the use of the large "visible" gas pump. The attendant would crank the pump handle and the gasoline would be pumped up into the top section, where the customer could view it through the large round glass housing to make sure it was clean gas. From the early days of gas engines up to the 1950s, gasoline was not processed as well as it is today, and it was known to have impurities at times that could cause an engine to malfunction.

In the 1910s, many towns and cities across the United States were seeing an increase not only in the sales of the automobile but in their repair as well. The Hollister Auto and Machinery Company was one of the many businesses that came about with the increase in automobile traffic in Hollister and San Benito County. They all wanted to offer the best possible service and product available at the time.

Designed by architect William Weeks just after the earthquake of 1906, Hollister's Masonic Lodge 211 was built at a cost of $21,000 at the corner of San Benito and Fourth Streets. Lodge 211 was formed in 1871 and rededicated on April 28, 2011, after extensive renovations using the same ceremony that George Washington used on the Capitol building. The prominent clock tower is featured on the City of Hollister's logo. A gathering that consisted of 90 people attended the event.

Hollister Steam Laundry is pictured with a partial view of the Willard Service Station on the left. Note the small banner hanging near the laundry entrance door indicating that it was "California Fiesta Year—Let's All Celebrate." The laundry building was built around 1925 and destroyed by fire in 1955.

The Savings and Loan Bank of San Benito County was established in 1892 by the Bank of Hollister, which was incorporated in 1873. In 1915, it had total resources of $1,225,381.46. Pictured from left to right are a Mr. Harris, William Hawkins, Dennis Paterson, Tom Hawkins (bank president) seated at the desk, and Cory Briggs. In 1916, they merged with the Bank of Italy, which eventually became Bank of America.

This wonderful bird's-eye view of a section of Hollister's business district was taken in January 1916. From the top of the county courthouse, the Brown and Chapple Hardware Company can be seen at the intersection of Fourth and San Benito Streets. The clock tower of the Masonic building is visible on the same side as Fourth Street, across from San Benito.

One of the largest and longest-lasting hardware companies on the central coast is Brown and Chappell Company. It dealt with hardware, builders' supplies, implements, vehicles, all accompanying lines, and large manufactures of sheet metal products. In this 1910 photograph, standing in the paint department from left to right are Steve Lavaynino, George Mann, unidentified, and Clarence McKee.

The metalware department of Brown and Chappell Company as seen in this c. 1910 photograph shows a wide range of items that were stocked, such as wood stoves, metal buckets, gasoline cans, washtubs, and much more. Hanging in the center of the ceiling are wire egg baskets, which, when not in use, could be folded almost flat for easy storage. The two clerks are unidentified.

This late-1920s or very early-1930s photograph shows the most modern of paint departments at Brown and Chappell Company, indicating it is a major "Jobber" for Dupont Paints, stains, and finishes. The clerk is unidentified. The original owners were Smith and Chappell. In 1896, C.M. Brown purchased Smith's interest, and from that time on, he and G.A. Chappell were the owners. The old, original tin ceiling is still intact in this photograph.

By the early 1950s, Brown and Chappell were still in business, but as seen in this photograph, the merchandise had changed from washtubs and tin buckets to electric skillets and electric floor heaters, all serving the needs of the modern shopper.

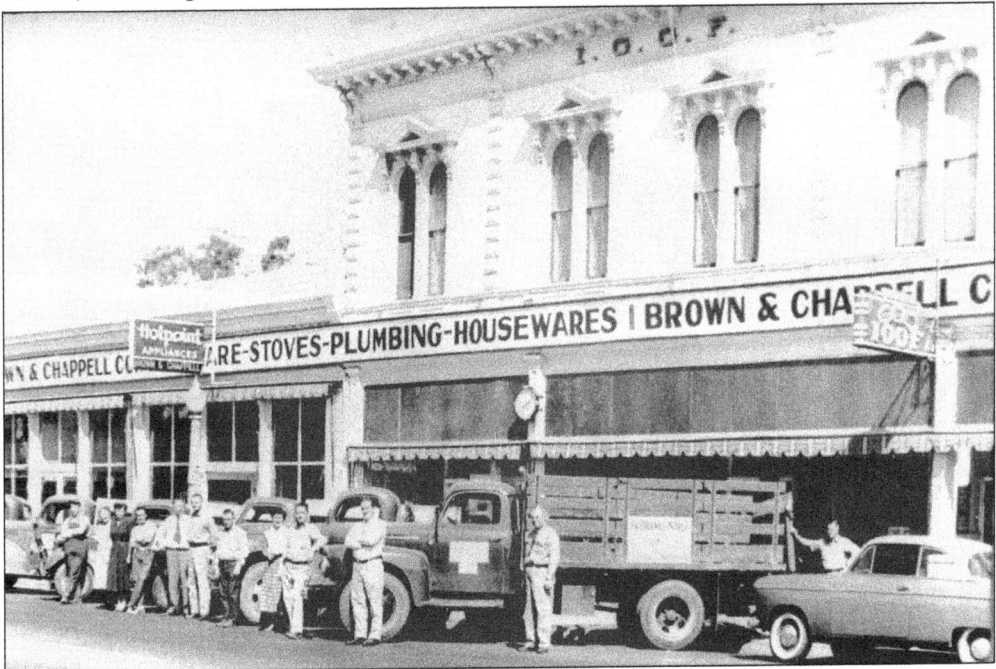

A very early-1950s photograph shows some of the drivers and staff from Brown and Chappell Company posing in front of the store, now offering Hotpoint Appliances. The firm of G.A. Chappell and Company of Gilroy carried the same lines and was owned by G.A. Chappell and C.M. Brown. While Brown was in charge of the Hollister store, Chappell handled the Gilroy business.

In this October 1888 photograph, the Hollister Transfer Company freight wagon is seen parked out in front of the local Wells Fargo and Company Express Office, which was located in the brick building. The building also housed other businesses, such as the San Benito Land Company and the Bendgard and Kleen Bar. Charles Shaw is seen leaning on the horse, while Bill Shaw leans on the wagon. Dan McCarty is seen in the driver's seat wearing his Wells Fargo hat. The others are unidentified.

Pictured here in 1884, the McMahon House Ball Club takes time out for a group photograph. From left to right are (first row) Ed Searls and Maurice Dooling, who went on to become a federal court judge of the First California District; (second row) Frank Hickock, John Fay (manager), and Ed Montgomery; (third row) Cory Briggs, Ed Nash, Charles Dowdy, James Kearny, and Reg Shaw.

Bob Butts tends the bar while Louis Danbinbus looks over a bottle of "Who Hit John" in this unidentified saloon photograph taken in the very early 1900s.

Karlyn Reisinger and Katerhyn Zgragen are pictured around 1945 hard at work behind the counter of Baywood Creamery, which was located on San Benito Street between South and Seventh Streets on the east side.

Baywood Creamery, or the Baywood Holstein Farm, had been active in the Hollister area for many years. With the advent of the automobile, it turned from the horse and wagon to a more modern mode of travel and delivery. Standing proudly next to his new truck in this 1927 photograph is driver Wes Brookshire. The two little girls are not identified.

The Hollister Telephone headquarters looks busy in this 1910 photograph. Hollister had its first telephone company in 1892 at 320 Fifth Street. There were telephones in only 52 other places in the state at that time. The first telephone company was known as the Sunset Telephone Company, and hotel manager Tom McMahon placed the first phone in the McMahon House. The office switchboard for this company in San Juan Bautista received all calls between San Francisco and Los Angeles. The first switchboard in Hollister was in Allison's Stationery Store in 1903. In 1913, the office was moved to 327 Fifth Street, and at that time, there were 198 telephone subscribers. In 1956, there were 3,500 in Hollister and the county. The operators in this photograph are not identified.

The Hollister Brewery Beer Hall is pictured with three unidentified men out front on the board walkway in this c. 1890 photograph.

The Hollister Rockdale Store was established in 1902. It was a cooperative general store patterned after similar stores in England. On a trip to England, Grant Button took notice of the cooperative style of doing business. When he returned to Hollister, he became the first manager of the new store, which seemed fitting, considering his experience (albeit limited). He is seated on the right behind the counter. Notice the long bar-looking object at the top of the photograph. This is a gaslight fixture, which was common at that time period for use along with electric power. On the back wall to the right (on shelves) are the old, reliable kerosene lamps with glass shades. The building was destroyed during the earthquake of 1906. The brick building fell into a pile, killing a woman who was living upstairs. It was replaced with a wood-and-stucco structure and continued to do business for a number of years.

In this December 1919 photograph of the interior of the Hollister Rockdale Store, the shelves are stocked to the brim with most anything one could need for everyday life. By this time period, most everything was electrified, but on the back wall up on the shelf, there are still kerosene heaters and lamps, which are used today by many in rural areas when the power goes out. Standing behind the counter from left to right are Ray Wheatcraft, L. Davis, Dena Neilsen, and Hap Huntsman. The customers are not identified.

This late-1910s or early-1920s photograph shows the interior of the Hollister Auto and Machinery Company. An Indian or Harley Davidson motorcycle is just visible in the bottom left-hand corner, just in front of the automobile. The boards near the bottom right of the photograph in the cement would have been removed to allow a mechanic to walk down into a pit to perform various repair tasks to automobiles, such as changing engine oil.

This early-1930s interior view of the India Tire Company shows a good selection of new tires ready to be installed. The automobile pictured inside is waiting its turn for service. The employees are not identified.

Tiffany Ford was founded in 1910 and recently celebrated its 100th year in business, making it the oldest Ford dealership in California and sixth oldest in the United States. Founded by E.W. Tiffany, it has followed the growth of Hollister and the community, keeping service and quality a top priority. Beginning in 1910, Tiffany sold four automobiles. He then sold seven in 1911, fourteen in 1912, twenty-eight in 1913, forty-eight in 1914, and sixty-three in 1915. From October 1, 1915, to February 15, 1916, he sold 16 cars, and that was considered the dull season. In 1914, San Benito County spent $300,000 for a system of improved roads, and the state had just completed a stretch of concrete highway through the county at a cost of $150,000. Pictured is a very early model of the new Thunderbird convertible.

Shown is another photograph of the San Benito Land Company office next to the Wells Fargo Office. The African American is identified as Bruce. The man standing on the sidewalk with two little boys on either side of him is A.M. Cumming, a local grocer. On his right is a Mr. Sanford, a local butcher, and the town marshal B.F. Ross. The two small boys in white shirts are Tom and Joe O'Donnell. The two men in the doorway with Derby hats are John Bengard and Henry Kleen, who were saloon proprietors in the building. The man on the right of the flagpole in the rear without a hat is Ambrose Butts. The building was located at Fourth and San Benito Streets.

This 1910 fire destroyed a half-block building at the corner of Sixth and San Benito Streets. Included in the burned businesses were Cox's Clothing Store, Graham's Meat Market, the Radcliff Grocery, Reinhart Candy Store, Mrs. Gruff's Millinery Store, and the Crosby Saloon. The earthquake of 1906 destroyed the two-story Masonic Temple, which stood on the corner, and two days later, the north wall collapsed onto Graham's Meat Market. The one-story building had replaced the buildings damaged four years earlier.

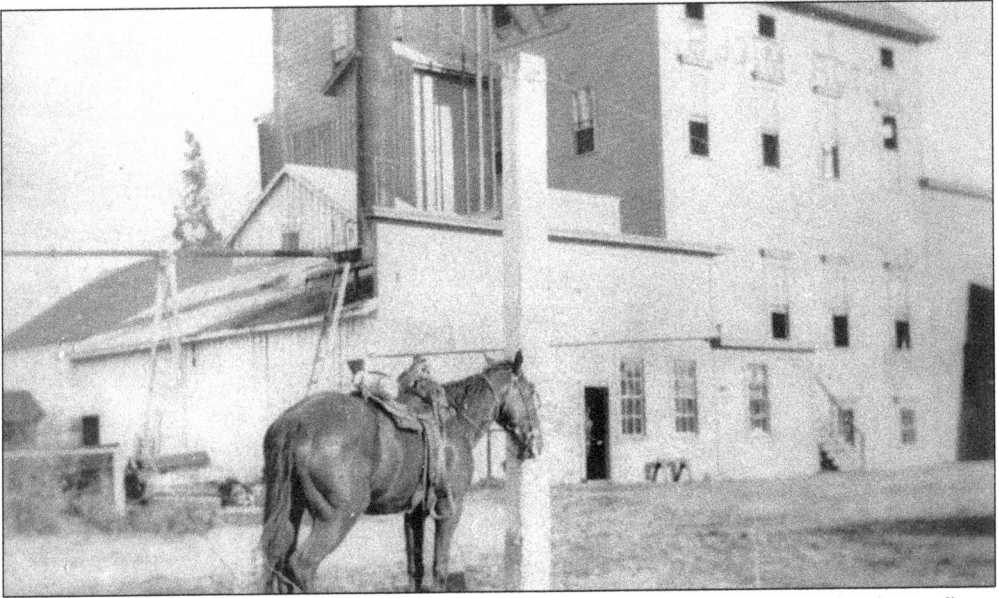

This 1891 photograph was printed in reverse, as indicated by the lettering just under the roofline, which should read "Victor Mills." The building was an early-day landmark and stood on the site that is presently home to the Hollister Canning Company. Constructed in 1880, it began as the Central Milling Company and was owned successively by Victor Mills, the Sperry Flour Company, and the Bolton Dried Fruit Company before its purchase in 1916 as the first Hollister Canning Company plant. At its peak of production, the mill turned out 450 barrels of flour a day. None of the original building remains, as the upper floors were dismantled and the ground floor was destroyed in a fire.

In the late 1870s or early 1880s, the Hollister Volunteer Fire Department posed for this photograph, showing off what items of uniforms it had as well as the new brick firehouse. Notice that the fireman second from left is holding what would be the company's fire trumpet, or horn, which was used to amplify the chief's voice while calling out orders during a fire call. The little wooden building, partially hidden by the tree, is where the justice court was conducted. At the far left is the Alhambra House, which extended to the corner of San Benito and Fifth Streets and included Kelly's Corner Bar. Oddly enough, the Alhambra burned in the late 1890s, claiming the life of one man. Kneeling in the first row are Louis Stevens (left), Tom O'Donnell Sr. (second from left), Barrett McCroksey (eleventh from left), R.P. Lathrop (twelfth from left), and Art Shaw (thirteenth from left).

Fireman Jack Douglas proudly sits behind the wheel in Hollister's first fire truck in 1915.

Pictured is the Alpine Creamery with workers visible in the open-ended building. The old Del Monte Packing Shed is seen in the background behind the water tank.

Two unidentified workers tend to beer making at the old Hollister Brewery, which was owned by Susan Varcol from 1874 to 1875. It was then sold to a Mr. Steinacher, who owned it until about 1890, when Adolph Wahl purchased it and changed the name to Wahl Brewery. His newspaper ads of the day indicated he produced the finest steam and bottled beer, and "when one would want an excellent drink, call for Hollister Beer."

In 1906, the Hotel Hollister was one of the town's leading hotels. Bruce Hickney, who had been in the hostelry business in Ellensburg, Washington, managed the Bank Grill before coming to Hollister around 1914 to take charge of the Hotel Hollister, which had been remodeled and modernized. It had 40 rooms, a large lobby and dining room, a billiard room, and a café.

Hollister had several breweries, which were well known for the fine beer they brewed. Here, Adam Renz is filling small oak beer kegs from a large fermenting barrel. It is thought that this is the inside of the Palmtag Brewery.

In this c. 1900 photograph of a local saloon interior, the barkeep is fashionably dressed to receive customers and serve them their favorite libations. Among their choices of beer is the Pajaro Brewery, as indicated on the advertising "give-aways" hanging on the wall on the right next to the bar. William Palmtag owned the Pajaro Brewery. On the left side against the wall sits two early slot or gaming machines. Notice the extravagant but decorative ornamental stencils, or *papel picado*, hanging from the ceiling.

For this 1900 photograph, George Kane, owner of the Cosmopolitan Saloon, poses with family members while the young delivery driver, L.G. Timer, sits in the delivery wagon for the French-American Bakery, owned by Joseph Mouesca. On the right side of the building, a partial advertisement is visible for a laxative that was made up by George Wapple, Druggist.

Pat Dooling (left) and Joe Kiser (right) pose on the porch of the Hollister Creamery building with an unidentified man in this 1899 photograph.

The early days of aviation brought many small towns all over the United States their first look at the new "Aero-plane" or "Flying Machine," and Hollister was no exception. Seen here in 1911, famed aviator Frank M. Bryant (1875–1965) is seen with his Twin-Tractor biplane when he came to Hollister. It was said that Frank Bryant could get into almost any airplane and fly off. He was listed as one of the first members of the Early Birds of Aviations, an organization of pioneers who flew solo before December 17, 1916. On occasions, pilots like Frank Bryant would tour around the country, promoting aviation or special events and at times would offer the locals a ride in the plane for a nominal fee.

The land for the Cottage was originally bought from James Hudner in 1896, and Tom Wilson erected the building in the same year at the corner of San Felipe and Wright Roads. At the time, the Cottage was a two-story affair, and the operator lived upstairs. This building burned down in 1906, and the present structure replaced it later the same year. The current building is a one-story construction with porches on the east and south that are protected by wooden awnings. As was popular in those times, it was of false-front architecture. A flagpole surmounted by a weathervane ornamented the top center of the building. The bar and mirrored back bar, with its pillared canopy, were bought from the Alvado Saloon on Fifth Street in Hollister. In 1956, the property was sold to Ray Dassel, who converted the bar into an office for his butane/propane business. The Dassels gave the bar to the San Benito County Historical Society, and it was moved to the Historical Park in Tres Pinos on October 9, 1995. It has since been completely restored and outfitted and is one of the very rare corner-entrance saloons known still in existence.

A group of local businessmen stands outside Wapple's Drugstore on San Benito Street during a wet winter day in the c. 1900 photograph.

R.K. Dunham (right), standing in the doorway, and the barber whose shop is located next to his merchant tailor shop pose along with a few customers in this c. 1895 photograph. A local news advertisement of the day stated that suits could be made from $20 and up, and pants could be made for $5 and up. "Cleaning and dyeing a specialty, all work warranted and a perfect fit guaranteed or money refunded." The shop is next door to the Granger's Union Building on San Benito Street.

Nash Corwith Briggs Jr. stands in front of his book and stationery shop at the corner of Fifth and San Benito Streets with his hands tucked in his trousers in this 1895 photograph. He was around 30 years of age at this time. His father, Nash Sr., was a prominent local attorney.

Hollister's first library is shown in 1905 with Olive Evans Hawkins standing in the doorway. She was the first librarian. The building was located where the city hall is now presently located on West Fifth Street.

In 1904, the Fraternal Brotherhood Lodge gathered to take part in a local parade at Fifth and Monterey Streets. Lucille Agnew is standing on the float, and Pete Daly is driving the team. The magnificent Victorian home in the background is still standing and is part of the historical walking tour that is conducted regularly in Hollister.

The Hollister Band was organized around 1910 and performed for several years for all occasions, including the Fourth of July and Portuguese celebrations. Band members from left to right are (first row) Dan Rezendes, John Bisho, Domingo Machado, Frank R. Machado, Frank Machado, Joe Cardoza, Tony Silva, and Manuel Enos Souza; (second row) Manuel DeRosa, Joe Velho, John Cardoza, Tom Silva, John Reno, George Pacheco, Bob Shaw, Louis Olave, Manuel Bettencourt, and Joe Freitas.

Another popular local orchestra in the 1920s was Lynn's Lightning Ladds. They were one of the most sought-after orchestras in the area during that time. Shown from left to right are (first row) Charles Gibson, Eddie Marentis, and Babe Lagenette; (second row) Joe Bernstein, Baxter Mead, Wright Lynn, Cliff Peterson, and Kope Kaiser.

The Eagle Drum Corps is seen marching down San Benito Street during a celebration in front of Penny Wise Drugs in this late-1940s photograph.

Before World War II, a local motorcycle group, the Salinas Ramblers, in conjunction with the motorcyclists of San Benito County, sponsored motorcycle hill climbs and dirt-track races out at Bolado Park and in Hollister at Legion Park. In this photograph, a member of the Modesto Motorcycle Club receives a trophy for placing in an event in July 1940 at Legion Park.

Each year, several thousand people would come into the Hollister area to watch and take part in the "Gypsy Tour" motorcycle events. These events drew large crowds, and with each subsequent year, the event grew. This July 7, 1940, photograph, taken at Legion Park, shows one of the drill team members receiving a trophy for winning an event.

The Gypsy Tour began in the late 1920s with a few motorcycle enthusiasts who would gather whenever they could, just to ride the open roads. Three members of a motorcycle drill team are pictured during a July 1940 evening event, probably at Legion Park in Hollister.

On July 7, 1940, Ed Kretz Sr. (number 38) and Mario Stillo (number 35) received their winning trophies during the Pacific Coast Championships, which were held at Bolado Park. The others are unidentified. Several local riders, including Johnny Lomanto and Paul McCann, participated heavily and became national champions, as did Sam Reno of San Jose in the hill climbs at Bolado Park. Johnny Lomanto was also one of the original members of the Hollister Top Hatters Motorcycle Club.

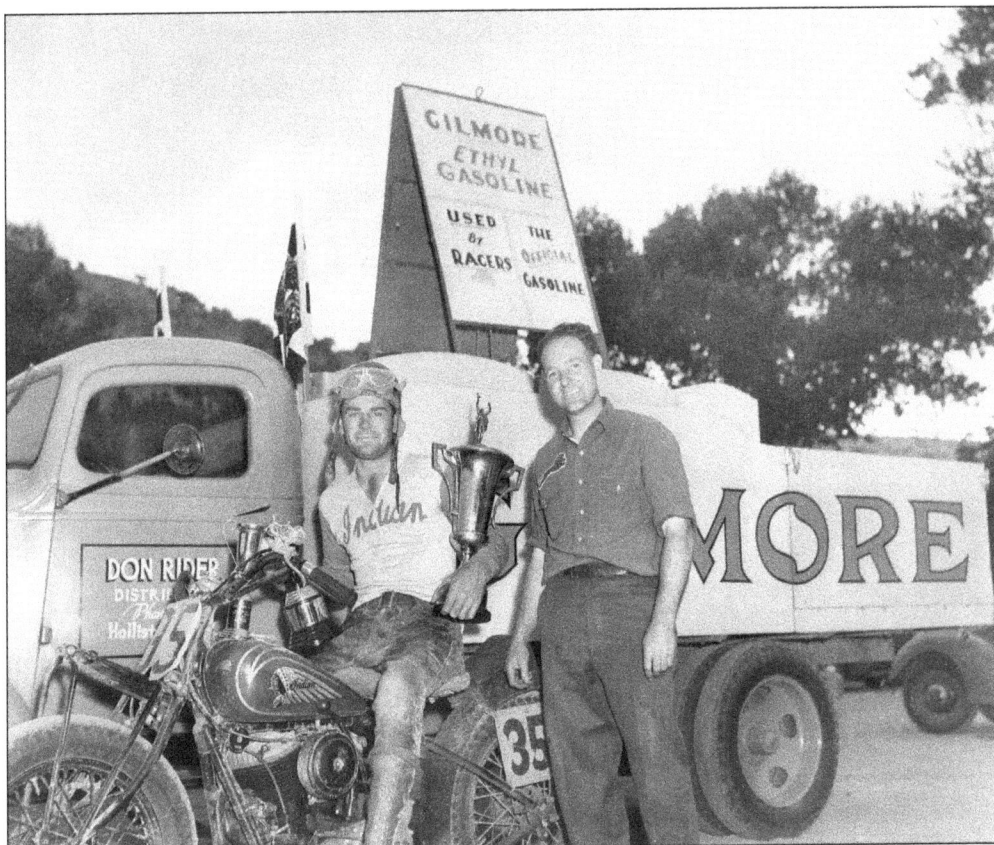

With the outbreak of World War II, most of the old motorcycle events were called off, and a good deal of those who rode went off to war. Number 35, Mario Stillo, and Don Rider, a local gasoline distributor, pose with the trophies they won over the three-day motorcycle event on the Fourth of July weekend in 1940 in Hollister.

The Gypsy Tour staged various motorcycle events in Hollister, and entrants from all over the nation would register to compete. Stunt-riding teams were in abundance, and competition could be heavy. On the Saturday night of the event, downtown Hollister was alive with people from all walks of life, enjoying a lighted parade down San Benito Street. Seen here are members of the Modesto Motorcycle Club.

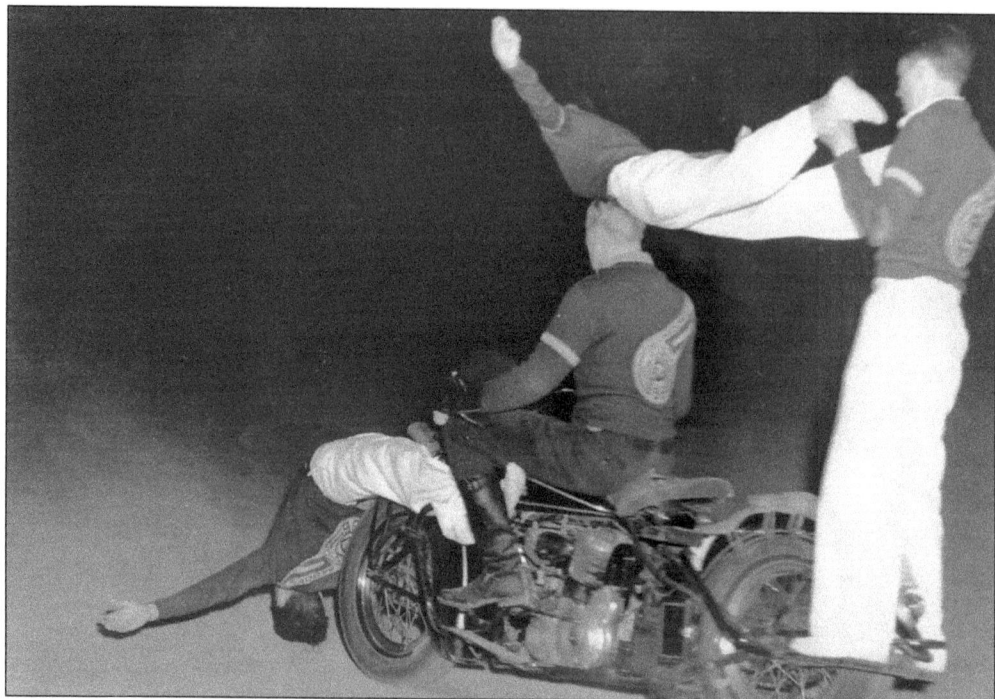

After World War II, everyone was eager to get back to whatever normal life was like before the war. That included sporting activities such as motorcycle events. The plans to revive the Gypsy Tour were set for the Fourth of July 1947, and local businesses were happy with the anticipated extra revenue. One might say it was the beginning and the end, all at one time. The Modesto Motorcycle Team is pictured competing.

By Friday of that weekend, several thousand motorcyclists had ridden into the town of Hollister, which, at that time, had a population of 4,500. The races continued at both Bolado and Legion Parks, and other various events were planned, such as a large, lighted parade for Saturday evening down San Benito Street. A large dance was to be held at the Elks Lodge. The San Francisco Motorettes are pictured here on the evening of July 7, 1940.

At some point on Saturday, the extra-large crowd of motorcyclists began sort of an exhibition all their own with some "spinning donuts and burning rubber" on San Benito Street. Several local boys, like Gil Armas and Jim Cameron, who were members of the original Boozefighters, a motorcycle club from Southern California, were credited—along with others—of riding into some of the bars, such as Johnny's, and parking their bikes inside. Seen here receiving a trophy are the San Francisco Motorettes.

Some other businesses also had a few visitors enter their establishments in this unconventional method. Some local cowboys on horseback did not want to feel left out, so they made a grand entrance on their horses in a few of the bars, just to keep things even. The San Francisco Motorettes are presented a trophy.

The New Deal Café, now known as Johnny's, was named for the character that Marlon Brando portrayed in the film *The Wild One*. It became famous as the center of the motorcycle event.

At this point, San Benito Street was at a standstill. The seven-member police force had blocked off both ends of the roadway and was trying to keep a lid on the action with the assistance of the California Highway Patrol. Two members of the Modesto Motorcycle Club receive an award at Legion Park.

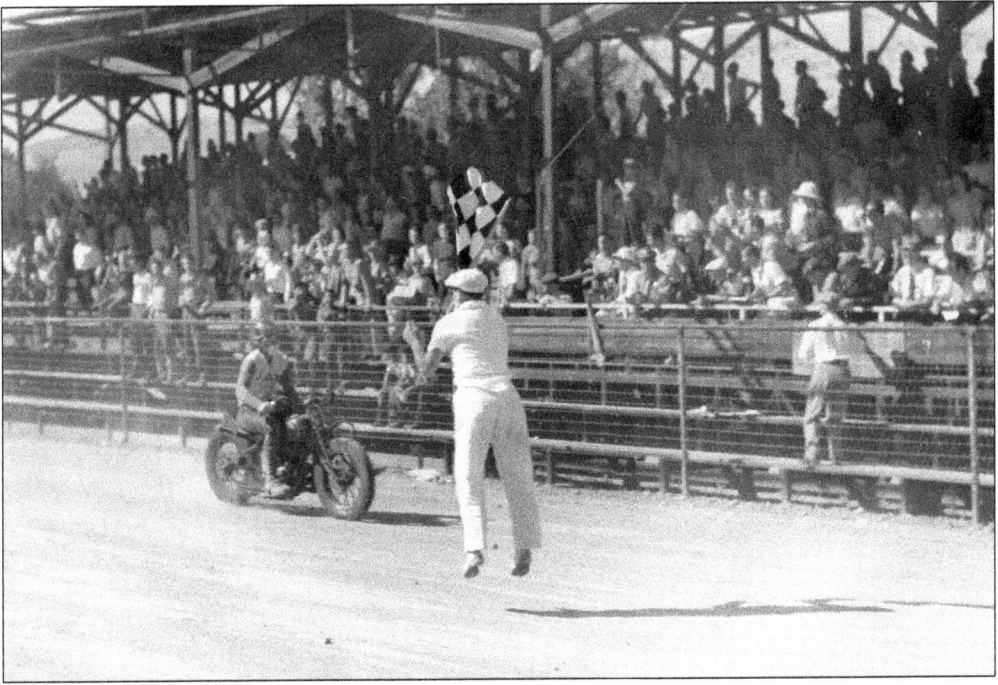

On a Saturday night in July 1947, the curb areas in downtown were tightly packed with motorcycles, but the large crowds of people hid them from view. A checkered flag is waived as number 35 crosses over the finish line at Bolado Park.

Comfortable sleeping spots were scarce, so participants slept on lawns and in the streets. The national news media reported that Hollister had become a pit of drunkenness and vice, but many locals reported that things were never as bad as had been reported. Mario Stillo (number 35) of Chico crosses the finish line at Bolado Park.

When the event ended, 50–60 individuals had been arrested for public drunkenness, disorderly conduct, and reckless driving. The same number had been injured trying to have fun. In this photograph, one of the racers at Bolado Park begins to lose control of his bike on a straightaway.

By mid-day Sunday, headaches and sore bodies were ready to hit the road and head home. Number 51 goes down on the track at Bolado Park.

In this Fourth of July 1947 photograph, bikes are lined up along the sidewalk in front of the First National Bank at Fifth and San Benito Streets with crowds of locals trying to get a look at what was going on. The single motorcyclist sitting on his bike in the lower right corner is being counseled by Fred Earle, Hollister police chief, while California Highway Patrol officers stand by with tear-gas guns. The Holland Club Bar is the business in the middle of the photograph and was another major location of activity.

Pictured from left to right are Archie Betts, Charley Garcia, Louis Tyler, Frank Gruves (of the California Highway Patrol), and Jack Wright (from Salinas Police Department). Gene Patterson from the Hollister Fire Department is looking on. The community, as with most in the first few years after the end of World War II, desired mostly to regain some sense of normality. Such was the case in Hollister, with its plan to bring back the very popular motorcycle events, which would bring in needed income for the locals as well. At the same time, on that weekend of a new era, the events that were planned as a positive movement forward were deeply tarnished, looked upon nationwide as something totally negative. Due to the hyped-up press, these events thereafter never flourished as they once did prior to World War II.

What began as an effort to revive the Gypsy Tour and bring back all the prewar events got off to a rocky start but continued as a major motorcycle event for many years. Racers at Bolado Park prepare to cross over the finish line at the dirt track.

When the 1953 film *The Wild One*, starring Marlon Brando and Lee Marvin, was released, the public began to think that all bikers were nothing but drunken misfits and sociopaths. During the years that followed, thousands of motorcyclists would descend on Hollister for the Fourth of July to ride and show their cycles. This event was cancelled in 2009, when the economics of such a large event became unmanageable. In this early photograph, a racer rounds one of the corners at Bolado Park.

Mark E. Gardiner wrote an article for a now-defunct website (Classic Biker) and probably summed it up best: "Ironically, the sensational media coverage of the Hollister event helped spawn truly criminal 'outlaw' bike gangs. By the 1960s, clubs like the Hell's Angels made Marlon Brando look very innocent. The American Motorcyclist Association has been fighting a public relations rearguard ever since." In this photograph, a racer slams into a wooden fence at Bolado Park, ending his day.

Today, the Gypsy Tour is not a sanctioned event due to financial losses over the past seven to eight years, but several groups are hoping to bring it back. Every Fourth of July, hundreds of motorcyclists still come into Hollister and stop at Johnny's for refreshments and food. Groups come and go during the few days, riding the beautiful back roads of San Benito County and gathering to talk about the "good old days." In this photograph, racers on the dirt track at Bolado Park pour on the speed going around a corner.

Five

PEOPLE

Over the last 150 years, Hollister has been the county seat and the only large town within county limits. It has been the trading center for a large area, much of which is sparsely populated. Hollister is the center of a large agricultural region, which produces and ships a large variety of crops, such as lettuce, broccoli, peppers, tomatoes, and a host of other row crops. Cherries, apricots, grapes, and walnuts are major orchard crops, and in the drier southern part of the county, hay is grown on many acres. In fact, Hollister is one of the largest hay-shipping points in California. The San Benito County High School football team even calls itself the "Hay-Balers." The southern portions of the county are home to large cattle ranches and the Pinnacles National Monument, founded in 1908 by Teddy Roosevelt, which remains a major tourist attraction.

For many years, Hollister remained a small community, until the rapid growth of the real estate market in the early 1990s brought major developers into the area. The population tripled rapidly, with most of these new residents becoming commuters to a growing Silicon Valley some 35 miles to the north. This population growth has resulted in a new diversity of people, which has given Hollister and its neighboring communities a more international vibe. Small-town values are still an important part of life in Hollister, but the advantages of the 21st century will continue to play a major role in the growth of the city in the years to come.

Benjamin Flint was born in Maine and came to the California goldfields in 1849. He wrote home to his family in New England and gave exciting news of the riches to be had in placer mining. His brother Dr. Thomas Flint and their cousin Llewelyn Bixby decided to join him. They traveled via ship by way of the Isthmus of Panama and upon their arrival in San Francisco headed immediately to the town of Volcano in Amador County to join Flint. With their Yankee instinct for business, the three young men soon gave up on mining and entered the cattle business.

Lucy Brown, sister of Col. William Wells Hollister, came west with her brother in the early 1850s. They had a herd of 4,000 sheep for breeding, wool, and meat and used these animals to start a successful business enterprise.

George Wapple was a respected druggist in town and at one point became the county treasurer. During World War I, Mrs. Wapple (Jane McCloskey) organized a fundraising drive to support an orphanage in Belgium. Her efforts did not go unnoticed, and when the Queen of Belgium visited San Francisco at a later time, Mrs. Wapple was asked to make the 75-mile trip to meet the queen, who thanked her in person. In the 1970s, the Wapple house became home to the San Benito County Historical Society and now houses part of its collections as well as various displays. It is also used for public meetings.

After a year and a half at Volcano, Llewelyn Bixby, pictured here, along with his cousins Dr. Thomas and Benjamin Flint, decided to take the considerable sum they accumulated from their business ventures back to Maine and return overland with sheep and cattle. The problem was how to get the gold dust safely back to the Philadelphia mint. They had special buckskin jackets made with compartments in the linings, but that turned out to be too heavy. The boat going back was not full, so they decided to take an extra cabin. They put the gold between the mattresses and at least one of the three stayed in the cabin at all times. They arrived back in Maine in 1853, and after several months of planning, they returned to California. As they crossed the United States, the Flints and Llewelyn Bixby organized the firm of Flint, Bixby and Company. With careful buying, they accumulated 1,034 head of sheep and six yoke of oxen. By the time they reached Warsaw, Illinois, it was time for shearing, and they reaped an early return on their investment, with the wool bringing in $1,570.45. Once back in California, their investments continued to grow, which allowed them to purchase the Rancho San Justo near San Juan Bautista. This land was to become the present site of the town of Hollister.

Bertha Briggs was born in Hollister in 1874 to the San Benito County pioneer family of William and Delia Johnson. She taught school for several years around Hollister and then went to work for Coast Counties Gas and Electric Company for 15 years. She was always very generous in spirit as well with her gifts. She helped found the Native Daughters Children's Foundation, was a member of the Copa de Oro circle, and of the Native Daughters of the Golden West (NDGW) for 51 years, was grand president of grand parlor NDGW in 1921, was the first secretary of the San Benito County Chamber of Commerce, organized the Hollister Women's Club in 1914, and served three terms as president of the Hollister Business and Professional Women's Club. She organized the Girl Scouts in Hollister and served as treasurer for 40 years. She donated two scholarships to San Benito College and gave an electric organ to the Methodist church. The original Hazel Hawkins hospital benefited from her gifts with a complete stand-by electric plant. She also provided two dogs for the Seeing Eye foundation. Her love of community is still benefiting residents today through trust funds set up before her death.

This is a c. 1930 photograph of Georgia Wapple Frazer. Born in Hollister in 1912, she was the daughter of prominent Hollister druggist George Wapple. Because she was so involved with everyday ranching and farming activities, she developed a great appreciation for the 4-H programs, which needed support at the local county fair livestock auction. In her will, Georgia Frazer left $1-million gifts to four individual San Benito County organizations, among them the 4-H Youth Development and Eagle Scout Scholarship programs. She also left $25,000 to the San Benito County Historical Society, which operates its museum from her childhood home at 498 Fifth Street in Hollister. She passed away in Florida in 1992.

Hazel Hawkins, who died from appendicitis at the age of nine on March 5, 1902, was adored by her grandfather, prominent Hollister businessman Thomas Hawkins. After her death, he funded the construction of Hollister's first hospital and named it for Hazel Hawkins. He felt that if a hospital would have been available at the time she became ill, "Little Sunshine"—as he called her—might have recovered. The hospital was dedicated on November 13, 1907.

Hiram Pond (left), founder of Pond's Drugs, and an unidentified employee pose in front of the drugstore in this 1909 photograph. Pond had the store built on the west side of San Benito Street between Fourth and Fifth Streets after the earthquake of 1906 devastated the entire block. Pond is credited with originating the facial cream that women throughout the world have used. Claude McHenry bought the business in 1935, and it was later sold to Joseph Whalen, who renamed it Whalen's Drugs.

The Palmtag, Barg, and Kleen Saloon was photographed in 1900. The business was an agency of the Pajaro Brewery, which William Palmtag owned. He was born in Baden, Germany, on October 23, 1847, the son of Frederick and Christina, and was educated at Emmendingen, Baden, Germany. He came to California in 1864 and engaged in mining for six years. He went into the wholesale liquor business and was a wine merchant for 24 years.

Pictured is the interior of the Palmtag and O'Connor Saloon in 1895. William Palmtag served as president of the Hollister Creamery, vice president and part owner of the Hollister Water Company, director of the Hollister Cold Storage, treasurer for the Pines Warehouse Company and the San Benito Vineyard Company, and supervisor of San Benito County.

Pictured is the interior of the Palmtag Saloon before 1900. It was located at Fifth and San Benito Streets. William Palmtag acquired a large vineyard in the Cienega region of San Benito County in 1880. A Frenchman named Theophile Vache planted the vineyard in 1854.

William Palmtag (center), with his sister and Leopold Palmtag, poses at the Cienega Ranch. In 1891, William Palmtag became president of the Farmers' and Merchants' Bank of Hollister. In 1908, the name was changed to the First National Bank of Hollister. He also presided over the Hollister Savings Bank.

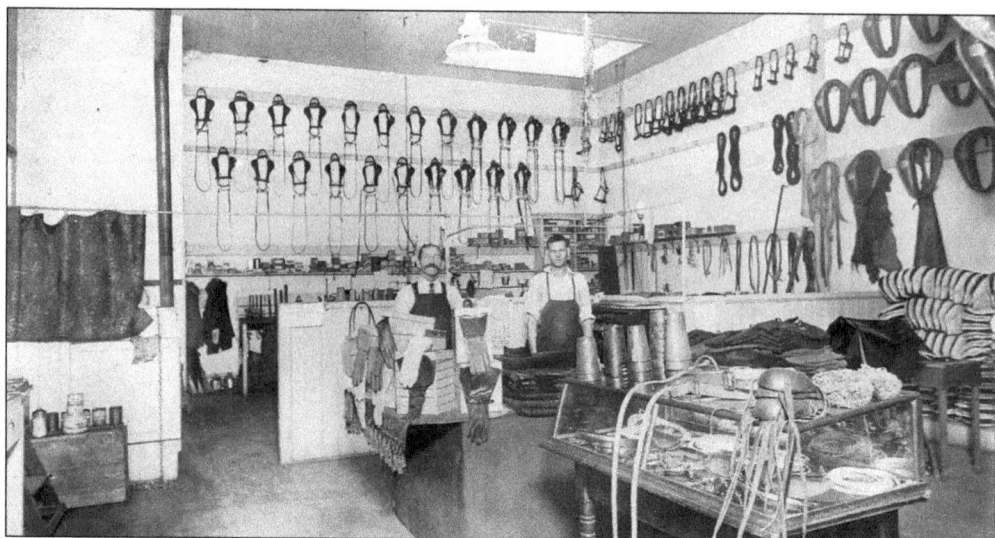

Pictured are George Hansen (left) and Andrew Hansen of Hansen Harness Shop in Hollister. It was located on San Benito Street between Fifth and Sixth Streets. This photograph was taken some time between 1914 and 1917. When World War I broke out, Andrew enlisted with the US Army Cavalry. He was stationed in Texas training troops. During the time he was gone, the business fell onto hard times, and his father was forced to close it down. When Andrew returned in 1919, he and his father began Hansen Equipment and Harness Company, selling International Farmall tractors and engines. They did business at the Fifth and Line Street location until the mid-1940s.

The Weibe Pick-Up Loader was manufactured in 1946. Walter Weibe is seen loading a grain bag onto the bed of the truck.

Walter Wiebe demonstrates his prototype Wiebe Fruit and Nut Harvester. The Wiebe Company designed and manufactured many farm implements as well as other devices used in everyday life. The Fruit and Nut Harvester did the work of 10 to 14 hand pickers and was self-propelled by a six-horsepower gasoline engine. Walter Weibe was born in 1909 in Paso Robles, California. In 1911, his family moved to Hollister, and when his father died in 1912, he became the man of the house.

Pictured is the Wiebe Manufacturing Company in 1944 at 1161 San Felipe Road in Hollister. The company's biggest success was the Wiebe Pick-Up Loader, which enabled two men to load sacked beans or other products onto a flatbed truck.

San Benito County cowgirls are ready to get into the action at the rodeo at Bolado Park in the mid-1930s. From left to right are Virginia Hargous O'Connell, Betty Regan Jones, Violet Penna, Evelyn Silveria Pivetti, and Mrs. Smyrle Shumway.

Sheriff Jerry Croxon was very well liked and respected, holding his position for over 20 years. He was extremely fond of horses and certainly sits the saddle well in this early-1900s photograph. He always participated in the various parades and fiestas that took place in and around Hollister and the nearby town of San Juan Bautista.

On July 4, 1893, Minnie Denver Turner is in charge of the four young ladies dressed in costume representing the C.L. Burns City Stables. Shown from left to right are Amy McPhail, Florine Rosenberg, Hazel Scott, and Tina Hendericks.

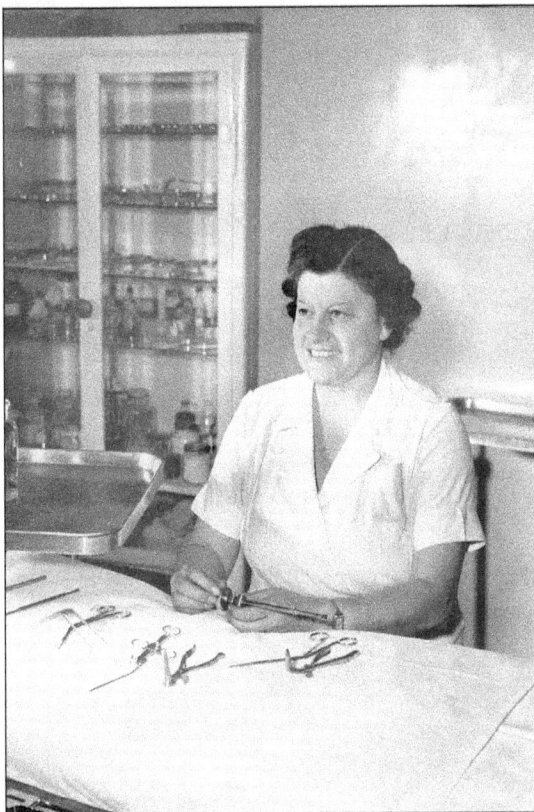

Around 1942, Hollister resident T3G Genevieve L. Penna of the Women's Army Corps (WAC) poses at her station for this photograph. One of her duties as technician was anesthetist in the operating room at the station hospital at 1st WAC Training Center, Fort Des Moines, Iowa. Her job was to prepare the instruments for operations. She was a graduate registered nurse at Hazel Hawkins Memorial Hospital and assistant superintendent of the hospital before joining the WAC.

The employees of the Bank of Italy (now Bank of America) pose in 1918 for this company photograph. From left to right are (first row) Miss Hasbrouck, T.S. Hawkins (president), and Eileen Hauser; (second row) Wirt Thomas, Jack Maxwell, Don Pendergrast, Warren Hawkins, Ed Cushman, and O.C. Willard; (third row) Thomas Flint, Warren McConnell, and Dennis Paterson. At the time of this photograph, the Bank of Italy had been in Hollister for two years. It merged with the Bank of Hollister in 1916.

Pictured in this early-1900s photograph are, from left to right, Nash Briggs (attorney), Cory Briggs (clerk), and Ransom Lathrop (merchant). All three men were very involved in the growth of Hollister.

Jack O'Donnell (left) and Dick Hill were two of the main founding members of the San Benito County Historical Society. Each spent thousands of hours not only developing a museum in the old Wapple House but also putting together the historical park at Tres Pinos, complete with a number of historic structures and a great deal of farm equipment. Thanks to both of these men and Fred LaSalve, the history of Hollister and San Benito County is preserved for many generations to come.

Pictured here is Joe McMahon (left) with Pat DeRose, owner of DeRose Vineyards, in a section of the 150-year-old historic vineyard that was planted by Theophile Vache in the late 1850s. William Palmtag purchased the vineyard in 1880 and began his winemaking business. It has been restored and replanted by the DeRose family, the current owners.

Pat DeRose is pictured talking about the history of one of the sections of the old vineyard, which he and his family rescued in the 1980s. They presently produce award-winning wines with a national following. The property is home to the world's largest covered wine cellar, and DeRose is noted as the oldest existing winery in California.

William Palmtag produced wines from this vineyard, which won silver medals at the 1900 World Exposition in Paris.

This phtograph shows the main residence on the grounds of Peitra Santa Winery. Built in 1905, it was designed for the Dickerson family by Burley Griffin, an associate of Frank Lloyd Wright. It has been a private residence and is presently used for special events by the Blackburn family, the present-day owners of the winery.

Pietra Santa Winery, established in 1985 by the Blackburn family, sits on a portion of the original Vache Vineyards. The oldest planting of Zinfandel grapes dates to 1905, and the present tasting facility dates to 2000. San Benito County is home to other world-class wineries, such as Calera, Leal, Guerra, Aimee June, and Jayse Wines.

Visit us at
arcadiapublishing.com

....

www.ingramcontent.com/pod-product-compliance
Lightning Source LLC
Chambersburg PA
CBHW050634110426
42813CB00007B/1807